EVERYTHING YOU NEED

*Essential Steps to a Life of Confidence
in the Promises of God*

BIBLE STUDY GUIDE | SIX SESSIONS

DR. DAVID JEREMIAH

with Dudley Delffs

Harper*Christian*
Resources

Everything You Need Study Guide

Copyright © 2020 by Dr. David Jeremiah

Published in Grand Rapids, Michigan, by HarperChristian Resources. HarperChristian Resources is a registered trademark of HarperCollins Christian Publishing, Inc.

Requests for information should be addressed to customercare@harpercollins.com.

ISBN 978-0-310-11183-2 (softcover)
ISBN 978-0-310-11184-9 (ebook)

All Scripture quotations, unless otherwise indicated, are taken from the New King James Version®. Copyright © 1982 by Thomas Nelson, a registered trademark of HarperCollins Christian Publishing, Inc. Used by permission. All rights reserved.

Scripture quotations marked NIV are taken from the Holy Bible, New International Version®, NIV®. Copyright ©1973, 1978, 1984, 2011 by Biblica, Inc.® Used by permission. All rights reserved worldwide. www.Zondervan.com. The "NIV" and "New International Version" are trademarks registered in the United States Patent and Trademark Office by Biblica, Inc.®

Scripture quotations marked nlt are taken from the Holy Bible, New Living Translation, copyright © 1996, 2004, 2015 by Tyndale House Foundation. Used by permission of Tyndale House Publishers, Inc., Carol Stream, Illinois 60188. All rights reserved.

Any internet addresses (websites, blogs, etc.) and telephone numbers in this study guide are offered as a resource. They are not intended in any way to be or imply an endorsement by HarperChristian Resources, nor does HarperChristian Resources vouch for the content of these sites and numbers for the life of this study guide.

HarperChristian Resources titles may be purchased in bulk for church, business, fundraising, or ministry use. For information, please email ResourceSpecialist@ChurchSource.com.

Published in association with Yates & Yates, www.yates2.com.

First Printing January 2020 / Printed in the United States of America

CONTENTS

"His divine power has given to us all things that pertain to life and godliness . . . by which have been given to us exceedingly great and precious promises, that through these you may be partakers of the divine nature . . ." (2 Peter 1:3–4)

"But also for this very reason, giving all diligence, add to your faith virtue, to virtue knowledge . . ." (2 Peter 1:5)

"Add . . . to knowledge self-control . . ." (2 Peter 1:6)

"Add . . . to self-control perseverance . . ." (2 Peter 1:6)

"Add . . . to perseverance godliness, to godliness brotherly kindness . . ." (2 Peter 1:6–7)

"Add . . . to brotherly kindness love . . . For if you do these things you will never stumble; for so an entrance will be supplied to you abundantly into the everlasting kingdom of our Lord and Savior Jesus Christ" (2 Peter 1:7, 10–11)

INTRODUCTION

The Bible reveals that God left no detail to chance when He decided to create human beings. The precision and perfection of our body's systems are without equal: our circulatory, digestive, immune, and muscular systems are all designed to sustain our life. Yet His care for us goes beyond the formation of our body. When God created the first humans, He gave them a beautiful garden, companionship, and a purpose. Rather than withdrawing from the world after its creation, God remained involved. Even after Adam and Eve sinned and had to be banished from the Garden of Eden, the Lord did not abandon them . . . and He has never abandoned us.

Today, we encounter all kinds of pressures in our society. We're living in unprecedented times . . . which bring unparalleled tension. Family pressure. Time pressure. Financial pressure. Pressure to compete and succeed by our culture's standards—at work, in school, in our community, and maybe even in our church. As believers in Christ, we are encountering pressures in our world that we have never had to face before. It all can cause us to wonder at times if God sees us in our situation . . . and if He is really with us in the midst of it.

Recently, I've been encouraged by a particular passage of Scripture, 2 Peter 1:3–11, that reveals God is not only *with us* in the midst of our crises but that He has actually provided us with *everything we need* to handle whatever life throws our way. This passage is one that I've known all my life. I've studied it and taught it for years. But in recent days, when I have been feeling under pressure, it has provided fresh air in my spiritual lungs. I have found that inhaling God's promises from this passage forces me to exhale the pressures of the world.

In this study, we are going to follow the trail of logic found in this passage to understand how God's divine power gives us everything we need—not half, or most, or even a lot— to live a life of godliness. We will do this by exploring eight essential character traits—each one built on the previous one—that God has provided to move us from where we are to where He wants us to be. These character traits are:

- **Diligence**—pursuing the Lord with all your heart
- **Virtue**—the sustaining joy of a God-pleasing life
- **Knowledge**—the accelerated growth that comes from knowing God
- **Self-control**—the skill of bringing your habits under the Holy Spirit's control
- **Perseverance**—the resilience that casts off discouragement
- **Godliness**—the mirror-image of Christ in your personality
- **Brotherly kindness**—friendliness that draws people to yourself and to Jesus
- **Love**—the essence of serving God and others

These eight qualities are indispensable for your life as a believer in Christ. They are like critical tools that God—the ultimate "trail master"—has given you to direct you along this long trail that we call life. These tools will guide you. They will empower you. They will help you move forward and not lose sight of your goal. They will nourish and sustain you when the pressures mount around you. And they are all available to you at any time!

Life's pressures won't get easier. But the promise is that you can move forward with confidence when you realize God has given you *everything you need*. So let's get started!

HOW TO USE THIS GUIDE

The *Everything You Need* video study is designed to be experienced in a group setting such as a Bible study, Sunday school class, or small group gathering. Each session begins with a brief "Welcome" section and opening questions to get you thinking about the topic. The group will then watch the video message from Dr. David Jeremiah and engage in a time of directed discussion. You will close each session with a time of personal reflection and prayer as a group.

During the week, you can maximize the impact of the study by engaging in the "Between-Sessions Personal Study" activities provided for that week. Treat each personal study section (*Know the Truth, Unpack the Truth, Walk in Truth*) like a devotional, using the material in whatever way works best for your schedule. Note that these personal study sections are not required, but they will be beneficial to you as you look at the eight essential qualities found in 2 Peter 1:3–11 and begin to apply them in your life. Beginning in session two, there will be an opportunity to share any thoughts, questions, or takeaways you have from your personal study.

Each person in the group should have his or her own copy of this study guide. You are also encouraged to have a copy of the *Everything You Need* book. Reading the book alongside the curriculum will provide additional insights and make the journey even more meaningful. To help you use both the book and this study, refer to the "For Next Week" section for a list of the chapters in *Everything You Need* that correspond to the following week's session.

Keep in mind the video, discussion questions, and activities are simply tools to help you engage with each week's lesson. Furthermore, as you go through the study, pray that God will help you to diligently "add to your faith virtue, to virtue knowledge, to knowledge self-control, to self-control perseverance, to perseverance godliness, to godliness brotherly kindness, and to brotherly kindness love" (2 Peter 1:5–7)—knowing that as you do, "you will be neither barren nor unfruitful in the knowledge of our Lord Jesus Christ" (verse 8).

Note: If you are a group leader, there are additional resources provided in the back of this guide to help you lead your group members through the study.

PREPARE FOR THE JOURNEY

Like a hiker in the wild, we sometimes find our-
selves stranded in the snow, caught in the storms,
and endangered by the trials of life. It's dangerous
to be ill equipped for the journey. When we haven't
packed the right gear, we're underprepared, over-
exposed, and at risk of the elements. That is never
God's plan for us. Like a divine Outfitter, He wants
to give us everything we need for the journey. He
knows how to equip us to be people of character,
able to face the ruggedness of the world with dignity
and strength. He furnishes all we need for every
condition. But we've got to turn from our meager
resources and embrace the ones He provides.

DR. DAVID JEREMIAH

WELCOME

If you have ever been on a hike, you know how difficult it can be to adjust to arduous terrain. One moment you're marching at a brisk pace on level ground . . . and the next you're climbing up a rocky path strewn with boulders and tree branches. Depending on where you hike, the weather can shift from a sunny, cloudless, picturesque sky to a torrential thunderstorm in a matter of minutes. This is why experienced hikers know to prepare for such possibilities ahead of time and carry in their backpacks everything they will need to survive and thrive on the trail.

Just think of some of the items that experienced hikers know to pack. For starters, they will make sure they have the proper footwear for the trail and, of course, outerwear that is appropriate to the climate, season, and locale. They know nothing is more uncomfortable than walking for miles in shoes that hurt their feet—and being too hot or too cold because they failed to pack the proper clothing is no fun either. They also make sure they have a backpack that has adequate storage and accessibility and comfortably fits their body type.

Experienced hikers know that water and food are essential even for short hikes. So they make sure to pack water bottles or carry a filtration system that allows them to treat the water they find in streams so their bodies will stay hydrated. They pack energy bars, trail mix, and other portable foods to fuel their bodies as they burn through calories. They carry a lightweight first-aid kit in case they need to treat an injury on the path. And, of course, they carry a compass, map, or reliable GPS device to help them stay on track to reach their destination.

The same is true for us as we set out on our "hike" and strive to live a life for Christ. We need to be equipped, nourished, and prepared for the journey ahead. Just as unexpected weather or rocky trails present challenges to hikers, our life is often filled with demands that burden us with pressure and stress. But we don't have to live in fear because God has provided everything we need for the task. We simply need to walk by faith in His promises.

SHARE

If you or any of your group members are just getting to know one another, take a few minutes to introduce yourselves. Then discuss one of the following questions:

- What items do you always take with you when you go on a hike, a campout, or even a road trip? Why are those items so important to have with you when you travel? When have you needed them and forgotten to bring them?

— *or* —

- What comes to mind when you think of being prepared for a journey, a meeting, a task, or even a goal you have set? When are times that you have found being prepared has paid dividends in your life?

READ

Invite someone in the group to read the following passage as everyone listens. Then turn to the person on your left and answer the questions that follow.

His divine power has given to us all things that pertain to life and godliness, through the knowledge of Him who called us by glory and virtue, by which have been given to us exceedingly great and precious promises, that through these you may be partakers of the divine nature, having escaped the corruption that is in the world through lust.

But also for this very reason, giving all diligence, add to your faith virtue, to virtue knowledge, to knowledge self-control, to self-control perseverance, to perseverance godliness, to godliness brotherly kindness, and to brotherly kindness love. For if these things are yours and abound, you will be neither barren nor unfruitful in the knowledge of our Lord Jesus Christ. For he who lacks these things is shortsighted, even to blindness, and has forgotten that he was cleansed from his old sins.

Therefore, brethren, be even more diligent to make your call and election sure, for if you do these things you will never stumble; for so an entrance will be supplied to you abundantly into the everlasting kingdom of our Lord and Savior Jesus Christ.

2 PETER 1:3–11

➢ According to this passage, what is the source that provides everything we need for a godly life? How do we access this source?

WATCH

Play the video for session one. As you watch, use the following notes to record any thoughts, questions, or key points that stand out to you.

NOTES

The life of faith is an adventure . . . and a challenge. But God wants you to reach your goal— and He has provided the tools you need to get there.

God's *divine power* is the source of our godliness—the ability to be like Him in how we think, feel, and act. We cannot achieve godliness through our strength but only through God's power.

God's *limitless power*—the same power that created the universe and raised Christ from the dead—is unleashed in our life when we turn to Jesus as Savior. It is also unlocked for us each day as we spend time in God's presence and study His Word.

God communicates His power through His "great and precious promises," which sustain us as we walk by faith. His promises are available to us every day through the Scriptures.

God wants us to participate in His divine nature in order to become more like His Son Jesus and less like the world. As we grow and mature in our faith, we become better equipped to fulfill the plans that God has for us to further His kingdom in this world.

The first tool that Peter states we need to "pack" is *diligence* (see 2 Peter 1:5). God has given us everything we need for godliness—but we have to work it out in our everyday life.

To cultivate diligence, we must develop the right *habits*. In Colossians 3:23–24, Paul provides four specific habits to develop diligence:

- Look around

- Look within

- Look above

- Look ahead

The challenge today is for you to recognize that God is your guide on this journey and receive the power He has promised to provide.

DISCUSS

Take a few minutes with your group members to discuss what you just watched and explore these concepts in Scripture. Use the following questions to help guide your discussion.

1. Why is it so important to rely on God's power as the source of our godliness? When have you attempted to live a godly life in your own power? What were the results?

2. How do God's promises empower us on a daily basis? What do we need to do to claim His promises?

3. How has God's power fueled your ability to live out His purpose? What does living out your purpose look like on a daily basis? How does this advance God's kingdom?

4. How would you define the word *diligence*? Looking back over your life, where have you struggled to be diligent in your walk with the Lord? Where have you been more consistent and seen your diligence contribute to your spiritual growth?

5. Do you agree that diligence requires the consistent practice of specific habits? Why or why not? What else contributes to the cultivation of diligence in your Christian life?

6. Based on Paul's words in Colossians 3:23–24, what are the four specific habits required to cultivate diligence? Which of these do you currently practice? Which one(s) could you cultivate as a new habit to grow in your faith?

RESPOND

As your group concludes this first session, review the outline for the video teaching and look over any notes you took. In the space below, write down the most significant point that stands out to you. What does it mean for you to diligently rely on God's promises to empower you?

PRAY

Conclude your time by sharing any personal prayer requests, and then pray for those requests as a group. Ask God to work in each heart as you rely on Him for everything you need.

BETWEEN-SESSIONS PERSONAL STUDY

Take the material you have covered this week to a new level by engaging in any or all of the following between-session activities. Each of the questions in this section will help you claim God's promises as you diligently seek to *know* the truth, *unpack* the truth, and *walk* in that truth. Before you begin, spend a few minutes reflecting on your thoughts from the first session, and then ask God to guide you and empower you through these exercises. Note that some may resonate with your current circumstances more than others, so pay attention to how you feel as well as to what you think. Be sure to record your thoughts or key takeaways, as there will be time for you to share any thoughts you want to discuss at the beginning of the next session.

KNOW THE TRUTH

As you seek to experience more of God's power in your life, keep in mind that nearly every biblical author mentions it as one of God's key attributes. Consider the following sampling:

God has spoken once,

Twice I have heard this:

That power belongs to God.

PSALM 62:11

Yours, O LORD, is the greatness,

The power and the glory,

The victory and the majesty;

For all that is in heaven and in earth is Yours;

Yours is the kingdom, O LORD,

And You are exalted as head over all.

1 CHRONICLES 29:11

[I pray] . . . that you may know what is the hope of His calling, what are the riches of the glory of His inheritance in the saints, and what is the exceeding greatness of His power toward us who believe, according to the working of His mighty power which He worked in Christ when He raised Him from the dead and seated Him at His right hand in the heavenly places.

EPHESIANS 1:18–20

➢ Paul uses the word *dunamis* in this passage in Ephesians, from which we get the word *dynamite*. God's power is so "explosive" that it had the ability to raise Christ from the tomb after the crucifixion—and *that same supernatural power resides in you today*! Why do you think God's power is consistently mentioned throughout the Bible?

➤ Why is it so important for you to recognize God's power in your life in order to live by faith?

➤ Looking back on your life, when have you experienced God's power in unexpected yet undeniable ways? What are the major events or situations where you have been a witness and a conduit of the same "divine dynamite" that Paul describes?

UNPACK THE TRUTH

When we put our trust in Jesus as our Savior, it unleashed the power of God in our life. Many times, however, the temptation is to look elsewhere for the source of our personal power . . . which often results in idolatry instead of focusing on what God has already given us. As Peter explains, "By his divine power, God has given us everything we need for living a godly life. We have received all of this by coming to know him" (2 Peter 1:3 NLT). Through God and His power, we have access to *everything* we need as we journey along in this life.

If you are not experiencing the full benefits of God's power, you might want to examine your connection and commitment to the Lord. Just as an electrician might investigate why a circuit is not conducting the electricity needed to power a lightbulb, seek to identify areas where your own "faulty wiring" might be blocking the way you receive and exercise God's light and power in your life. Begin to do this by reflecting on the key passage for this study found in 2 Peter 1:3–11. Note that when Peter talks about the knowledge of the One who called us (see verse 3), he has three areas in mind:

- We must know Jesus personally and have a personal relationship with Him.

- We need to grow in our knowledge of God's Word and the doctrines, truths, and realities of God.

- We must grow in our knowledge of God's commands, guidelines, and patterns in order to please Him with our godly lifestyle.

So spend a few moments assessing your life in regard to each of these three areas of knowing God. Here are a few questions to help with your personal assessment.

➤ Do you know Jesus *personally*? When did you make a commitment to follow Jesus alone and serve God? How would you describe your relationship with Him today?

➤ On a scale of 1 to 10, with 1 being "needs drastic improve-
ment" and 10 being "ready to teach Bible classes," how would
you rate your *knowledge* of God's Word? What is the basis for
your understanding of the doctrines, truths, and laws of God?

➤ How does your lifestyle and the way you live reflect God's
commands, *guidelines*, and *directives*? What needs to change
for you to align your behavior and habits with God's truth?

WALK IN TRUTH

In our modern culture, we are often conditioned to want more—
more money, more time, more possessions, more friends, more
vacations, more awards, more achievements, and the like. Rarely
are we encouraged to trust that we have *enough* in this life. Rarely
are we told by those in our world to rest in the security of knowing that we have *everything we need*.

However, when we have a personal connection with Jesus
and when we seek to get to know Him better each day—by
studying His Word, meeting with Him in prayer, and listening to
His voice—we experience the life of joyful abundance that Jesus

said He had come to bring (see John 10:10). We recognize God's power in our life and also come to understand the peace, security, and confidence that comes from trusting Him for everything we need.

With this in mind, review each of the categories below and describe (1) how you see God's power already at work in this area, and (2) what you would like to see happen as more of God's power is unleashed in your life.

Personal peace and daily attitude

Physical, mental, and emotional health

Money and financial stewardship

Home life and present living situation

Spouse and family relationships

Significant, trustworthy friendships

Work life and career plans

Church attendance and involvement

FOR NEXT WEEK

If you are reading *Everything You Need* as you complete this study, review chapters 1–2 ("The Promise" and "Muscular Faith"). In preparation for next week, read chapter 3, "Moral Excellence," and chapter 4, "Mental Focus." Use the space below to write any key insights or questions from your personal study that you want to discuss at the next group meeting.

Session Two

SURVEY THE TRAIL

God's divine power gives you what you need for a great life through the knowledge of Him who called us by His glory. In personal terms, this means His power is transmitted into your life by His living promises. But you have a role to play in this process through your actions and choices. With diligence, you must add virtue to your faith. But here's your next great step—now you must add knowledge to your virtue. Always grow in the knowledge of Jesus Christ.

Dr. David Jeremiah

WELCOME

When planning a journey, it's not enough to simply make sure that you have packed everything that you will need for the trip. Starting well is critical, but it is also crucial to *survey the trail* ahead so that you not only know where you are going but also the route that you need take to get there. Planning and packing are an important part of preparing well for the journey—but they are not the only parts. You have to look at the big picture and consider how you will maintain your sense of direction as you move toward your final destination.

Think of this again in terms of planning a hiking trip. To reach your destination safely, you need to look at the weather forecast to make sure you won't be caught in a torrential downpour or get stranded in a snowstorm. You will likely consult with other hikers who have recently traversed the same route or visited the same destination. You will definitely want to look at a map of the trail so you know what lies in store for you. If certain obstacles or challenges are ahead, it is better to know about them before they block your path.

Surveying the trail will also provide security and reassurance if the unexpected occurs. You know that you have thought through what you will need as well as what might be required in the event of an unpleasant situation such as getting lost, sustaining an injury, or suddenly feeling ill. While you cannot foresee every possible contingency, you can pack the basics that will equip you for a wide variety of possible scenarios. Being aware of what you need—and anticipating what you *might* need—will enable you to undertake your journey with confidence.

Our spiritual journey similarly benefits when we choose to survey the path ahead. As Jesus once said, "Suppose one of you wants to build a tower. Won't you first sit down and estimate the cost to see if you have enough money to complete it?" (Luke 14:28 NIV). Jesus urged His followers to look ahead and consider what was required to reach their goals. As we will see in this week's study, the next two items on Peter's list—virtue and knowledge—will likewise help us to "estimate the cost" and use the tools God has provided to help us reach the destination.

SHARE

Take a few minutes at the start of this session to go around the group and share any insights you have from last week's personal study. Then discuss one of the following questions:

- What steps do you take to "survey the trail" when planning for a journey, goal, or task? How have those preparations helped you?

— *or* —

- Why do you think Peter begins his list of characteristics to build a godly life with *virtue* and *knowledge*? How do those serve as a foundation?

READ

Invite someone to read the following passage while everyone listens. Then turn to the person on your right and answer the questions that follow.

Finally then, brethren, we urge and exhort in the Lord Jesus that you should abound more and more, just as you received from us how you ought to walk and to please God; for you know what commandments we gave you through the Lord Jesus. For this is the will of God, your sanctification. . . .

But concerning brotherly love you have no need that I should write to you, for you yourselves are taught by God to love one another; and indeed you do so toward all the brethren who are in all Macedonia. But we urge you, brethren, that you increase more and more; that you also aspire to lead a quiet life, to mind your own business, and to work with your own hands, as we commanded you, that you may walk properly toward those who are outside, and that you may lack nothing.

1 THESSALONIANS 4:1–3, 9–12

➤ Based on Paul's words in this passage, what does it take to please God?

➤ What does *sanctification* mean to you? How would you describe the process of sanctification that God is working in your own life?

WATCH

Play the video for session two. As you watch, use the following notes to record any thoughts, questions, or key points that stand out to you.

NOTES

It is important to have a plan and be prepared . . . but just starting well is not enough. We need to use the tools God has given us to *maintain* good habits throughout the journey.

Peter reminds us that in addition to diligence, we must add *virtue* to our faith (see 2 Peter 1:5). Virtuous believers lead lives of integrity, kindness, goodness, generosity, and graciousness based on their knowledge of God's Word.

Jesus is the epitome of true virtue—which often upset the religious elite because they knew His character was superior to their own. Jesus explained to them the secret to leading a virtuous life: relying on God as our source and pleasing God as our motivation (see John 8:28–29).

Just as Jesus desired to please God, we are called to make it our goal to please God. When we know God as a loving Father, the path of virtue we travel becomes a joy and an adventure.

We live virtuous lives not to gain our loving Father's acceptance (which we already have) but simply because we want to please Him by being an excellent steward of the life He has given us.

In 1 Thessalonians 4:1–3, 9–11, the apostle Paul lists three practical ways to lead a virtuous life:

- Live above the fray of our culture (verse 3)

- Love our faith family (verses 9–10)

- Lead a quiet life (verse 11)

In addition to diligence and virtue, Peter instructs us to add *knowledge* to our character qualities. To live as a disciple of Jesus will require us to take three steps:

- Follow Jesus

- Study Jesus

- Obey Jesus

God sent Jesus, the living Word, to serve as our example of moral excellence. He sent the Bible, His written Word, to provide us with the knowledge we need for godliness.

DISCUSS

Take a few minutes with your group members to discuss what you just watched and explore these concepts in Scripture. Use the following questions to help guide your discussion.

1. How would you define *virtue* as it pertains to a person's life or character?

2. Who has served as your personal role model for living a godly life of virtue? How has that person inspired you to live virtuously?

3. Why is living a virtuous life a joyful adventure and not an arduous burden? What makes the difference between the two?

4. How do the three practices that Paul lists in 1 Thessalonians 4:1–3 and 9–11 help us to lead virtuous lives? Which of the practices presents the greatest challenge to you? Why?

5. Keeping Peter's progression in mind, why do you suppose knowledge follows virtue? Shouldn't our knowledge of God and His Word come before virtue? Why or why not?

6. There are three "ingredients"—following Jesus, studying Jesus, obeying Jesus—needed for us to grow in knowledge. How does each one contribute to our knowledge of God and His ways? How does our knowledge become wisdom?

RESPOND

As your group concludes this second session, think about what point, idea, or phrase has jumped out at you and lingered in your mind and heart. Write down what you are taking away from this session and why you think it resonates with you at this time.

PRAY

Take a moment to share any personal prayer requests for which you would like the group to pray. As you pray for one another, thank God for what He is revealing and the ways He is using this study to help you and your group grow. Ask Him to empower you to lead a life of virtue and knowledge so that you might complete the journey He has set before you.

BETWEEN-SESSIONS PERSONAL STUDY

Reflect on the material you have covered this week by engaging in any or all of the following between-session activities. Each of the questions in this section will help you explore the character traits of *virtue* and *knowledge* as you seek to *know* the truth, *unpack* the truth, and *walk* in that truth. Begin by reflecting on your thoughts since the previous session, asking the Lord to guide you through these questions and exercises and bring you to a new understanding. Be sure to write down your thoughts or key takeaways, as there will be time for you to share any thoughts you want to discuss at the beginning of the next session.

KNOW THE TRUTH

The Gospels reveal that Jesus made it clear He had been sent by His Father, and pleasing His Father was the basis for His ministry on earth. In the passages listed below, notice what Jesus states about His ministry and how He encourages us to follow His example. In particular, note how He instructs each of us to grow in *virtue* and *knowledge* as we abide in Him.

> Then Jesus said to them, "When you lift up the Son of Man, then you will know that I am He, and that I do nothing of Myself; but as My Father taught Me, I speak these things. And He who sent Me is with Me. The Father has not left Me alone, for I always do those things that please Him."
>
> As He spoke these words, many believed in Him.
>
> Then Jesus said to those Jews who believed Him, "If you abide in My word, you are My disciples indeed. And you shall know the truth, and the truth shall make you free."
>
> *JOHN 8:28–32*

> "Do not let your hearts be troubled. You believe in God; believe also in me. My Father's house has many rooms; if that were not so, would I have told you that I am going there to prepare a place for you? And if I go and prepare a place for you, I will come back and take you to be with me that you also may be where I am. You know the way to the place where I am going."
>
> Thomas said to him, "Lord, we don't know where you are going, so how can we know the way?"
>
> Jesus answered, "I am the way and the truth and the life. No one comes to the Father except through me. If you really know me, you will know my Father as well. From now on, you do know him and have seen him."
>
> *JOHN 14:1–7 NIV*

➤ What did Jesus say was necessary for people to become His disciples? How does this require attaining both virtue and knowledge?

➤ Why do you think Jesus identified Himself to both His followers and His critics by explaining His relationship to God? Why is knowledge of the relationship between Jesus the Son and God the Father so important to your own faith journey?

➤ How has following Jesus' example made it easier for you to live a life of virtue? How has it made your life more challenging?

UNPACK THE TRUTH

During this week's teaching, you discussed how the apostle Paul reveals three practical ways to lead a virtuous life and please God:

> Finally then, brethren, we urge and exhort in the Lord Jesus that you should abound more and more, just as you received from us how you ought to walk and to please God; for you know what commandments we gave you through the Lord Jesus.
>
> For this is the will of God, your sanctification: that you should abstain from sexual immorality. . . .
>
> But concerning brotherly love you have no need that I should write to you, for you yourselves are taught by God to love one another; and indeed you do so toward all the brethren who are in all Macedonia. But we urge you, brethren, that you increase more and more; that you also aspire to lead a quiet life, to mind your own business, and to work with your own hands, as we commanded you.
>
> 1 THESSALONIANS 4:1–3, 9–11

These three ways of leading a virtuous life can be summarized as *living above the fray of cultural immorality, loving others within the family of God,* and *leading a quiet life.*

Let's unpack each of these concepts. First, we can't live virtuous lives without adhering to God's standards for moral and sexual purity. Human nature has not changed from Paul's day to our own. In his time, as in our own, sexual immorality ran rampant in the culture. However, God made it clear—from the beginning of Creation—that such behavior does not reflect His will or plan for His children's lives (see Genesis 2:23–25; Matthew 19:4–6). God is pleased when we reject the world's immoral practices and instead choose to live virtuously by His standards. This is the essence of moral purity and personal virtue.

Second, we please God by displaying His love in our earthly relationships. Paul was known as the "apostle to the Gentiles" for good reason. He traveled through Macedonia, Greece, and Italy, among other places, sharing the gospel message of Christ and founding churches. Most believers in these new churches had not met before. They did not necessarily have much in common with one another other than their faith in Christ. But with this bond in place, they grew in their love for one another, displaying God's love for all people.

Third, Paul urges us to lead a life of quiet confidence in God's power, sovereignty, and goodness. When we place our trust in Christ, we do not need to be victims of circumstance, constantly worrying about the ups and downs of life. We can live with a sense of security that allows us to be an example to others— showing them that God provides everything we need.

Spend a few minutes reflecting on these three methods of leading a virtuous life. Use the questions below to help with your personal assessment.

James writes, "Submit to God . . . resist the devil and he will flee from you" (James 4:7). Five practical ways that you can submit to God and resist the devil include:

- *Fill your heart with Jesus:* Make it the greatest ambition of your life to please God. If you are driven by this motivation, it becomes much harder to fall into sin. Simply fill your heart with the desire to always please God.

- *Fill your mind with Scripture:* When you take the Bible and submerge it into your brain, it has a way of displacing other thoughts—and this pleases God. One way of accomplishing this "submersion" is by meditating on passages of Scripture that compel you to lead a life of purity and integrity.

- *Fill your routines with rules:* As a follower of Christ, you must set rules, establish boundaries, and create a lifestyle that will keep you from undue temptation. So set rules for yourself and establish guardrails for your life.

- *Fill your friendships with accountability:* God has given you everything you need for life and godliness, which includes other people. So find someone with whom you can be accountable and honest. Make a pact with that friend to hold each other accountable and live in holiness.

- *Fill your soul with resolve:* Do whatever it takes to free yourself from temptation. If it takes counseling, get it. If it takes giving up your electronics, give them up. Do whatever it takes! Don't wait another day!

Check each of the methods that you are currently practicing in your life and make a note about what you specifically do to safeguard your virtue. Also note the methods you are not currently practicing and write down how you could incorporate them into your daily life.

METHOD	HOW YOU CAN USE THIS TO SAFEGUARD YOUR VIRTUE
➤ Fill your heart with Jesus	
➤ Fill your mind with Scripture	
➤ Fill your routines with rules	
➤ Fill your friendships with accountability	
➤ Fill your soul with resolve	

➤ What does it mean for you to love others in your family of faith? How involved are you in local ministries? How actively do you participate at your church? How do others in your study group know you love them?

➢ Reflect on Paul's admonition to live a quiet, confident, peaceful life. How would you describe your current season of life? Where do you need to slow down, unplug, and refocus your priorities? What action can you take today that will move you in this direction?

WALK IN TRUTH

To live virtuous lives that please God, we must be committed to connecting our *head knowledge* with our *heart knowledge*. Intellectual knowledge is important, but unless we put our knowledge into action, it won't help us grow in our faith. When Peter used the words *know* and *knowledge* in our key passage, he understood them to mean an intimate and personal awareness that is anchored deep in the heart. This is the kind of knowledge that makes us long for the Savior and grow in our love for Him— the kind Paul mentions in Philippians 1:9: "This I pray, that your love may abound still more and more in knowledge."

Before your next group session, make a plan for connecting your head knowledge with heart knowledge. This plan might be to help teach at your church, serve in your community, or spend a day alone in silent retreat with God. You might feel compelled to meet a friend or acquaintance for coffee, prepare a meal for a family in need, or anonymously provide resources for someone getting back on their feet. Ask the Holy Spirit to guide you as you seek to turn your knowledge into action to create a spiritual practice. No one needs to know about the practice you choose except you and God!

FOR NEXT WEEK

If you are reading *Everything You Need* as you complete this study, read chapter 5, "Personal Discipline," in preparation for next week. Use the space below to write any key insights or questions from your personal study that you want to discuss at the next group meeting.

Session Three

STAY THE COURSE

True freedom is impossible without constraints. This may seem like a paradox, but when we abandon self-control and follow our cravings, what appears to be freedom becomes a form of servitude. We become slaves to our appetites. Self-control means imposing limitations so we can focus on our goals. It's a make-or-break discipline, the difference between success and failure in living a godly life.

DR. DAVID JEREMIAH

WELCOME

One of the joys of traveling is discovering little-known areas with unique sights or breathtaking vistas. Often these spots are only known to locals and require diversions from your planned route. Sometimes such spontaneous pursuits become dangerous, as you are forced to navigate off the beaten path or through treacherous wilderness areas. Suddenly, a spontaneous decision to detour in search of a hole-in-the-wall restaurant or to hike off trail to see a crystal waterfall turns into a frustrating mistake that leaves you lost and nowhere near your original destination.

As you journey on God's path, you will likewise encounter situations that will tempt you to take your eye off your goal. However, it's important to remember that while such detours from God's will may seem harmless enough, you are playing into the hands of an enemy who seeks nothing less than "to steal, and to kill, and to destroy" your life and your relationship with God (John 10:10).

Your enemy is committed to sabotaging you at every turn—and he will not hesitate to exploit any weaknesses he finds to achieve that goal. As James wrote, "Let no one say when he is tempted, 'I am tempted by God'; for God cannot be tempted by evil, nor does He Himself tempt anyone. But each one is tempted when he is drawn away by his own desires and enticed"

(James 1:13–14). James knew that if we fall prey to the enemy's schemes, we will end up off course pursuing goals that do not further the work that God has for us.

In life, it is important to recognize the inherent danger in straying off course. We must rely on the knowledge we have gained from God's Word and trust it more than our momentary feelings or perceptions of our environment. In other words, we need to grasp the next spiritual tool on Peter's list—and add "to knowledge self-control" (2 Peter 1:6).

SHARE

Take a few minutes at the start of this session to go around the group and share any insights you have from last week's personal study. Then discuss one of the following questions:

- When was the last time you got lost because you were distracted or took a side road to your destination? What prompted your unplanned detour? What impact did it have on the rest of your journey?

— *or* —

- How do you respond to the idea that you have an enemy who is seeking "to steal, to kill, and to destroy" your relationship with God? How does that reframe the way you think of distractions that take your attention away from what you know God is calling you to do?

READ

Invite someone in the group to read the following passage as everyone listens. Then turn to the person nearest you and answer the questions that follow.

I say then: Walk in the Spirit, and you shall not fulfill the lust of the flesh. For the flesh lusts against the Spirit, and the Spirit against the flesh; and these are contrary to one another, so that you do not do the things that you wish. But if you are led by the Spirit, you are not under the law.

Now the works of the flesh are evident, which are: adultery, fornication, uncleanness, lewdness, idolatry, sorcery, hatred, contentions, jealousies, outbursts of wrath, selfish ambitions, dissensions, heresies, envy, murders, drunkenness, revelries, and the like; of which I tell you beforehand, just as I also told you in time past, that those who practice such things will not inherit the kingdom of God.

But the fruit of the Spirit is love, joy, peace, longsuffering, kindness, goodness, faithfulness, gentleness, self-control. Against such there is no law.

GALATIANS 5:16–23

➤ Why is walking in the Spirit essential for self-control? What is the basis for exercising godly self-control? How does practicing self-control produce spiritual fruit?

➢ Do you agree that lack of self-control is ultimately a spiritual problem? Why or why not?

WATCH

Play the video for session three. As you watch, use the following notes to record any thoughts, questions, or key points that stand out to you.

NOTES

Peter's life illustrates how God can transform any person into the likeness of Christ. God remains focused on transforming His faithful followers into the likeness of Christ.

God's divine power has given us everything we need for this life—but we can't be passive about the process. As Peter states from his own experience in our key passage, we must diligently add to our faith, virtue, and to virtue, knowledge, and to knowledge, *self-control.*

Practicing personal discipline requires us to recognize three essential truths. The first truth is that we *must make self-control a priority.* Self-control helps us experience abundant life by compelling us to deny an immediate indulgence in order to accomplish a higher-level goal.

The second truth is that *self-control requires us to exercise maturity.* Our flesh is drawn to sin, but the Holy Spirit that dwells within us draws us to holiness. While the battle may exhaust us at times, we must remember we have already been set free.

The third truth is that *self-control deepens and strengthens our personal discipline.* This helps us stick to the path God has set for us, knowing we will please Him as we journey to our heavenly destination. Followers of Jesus know true freedom comes from living within God's boundaries.

Developing self-control requires a plan and a strategy. Toward this end, we can take five steps to gain greater levels of self-control:

- Ask for the Holy Spirit's help

- Adjust our thoughts to pleasing God

- Acquire new habits that exercise godliness

- Avoid tight spots where we're likely to be tempted

- Accept the process and turn back to God when we fall

DISCUSS

Take a few minutes with your group members to discuss what you just watched and explore these concepts in Scripture. Use the following questions to help guide your discussion.

1. What comes to mind when you think of self-control? Do you view yourself as a disciplined person? Why or why not?

2. Why is self-control such a vital part of our Christian life? Why do we often view it negatively or assume God just does "not want us to have fun"?

3. Paul wrote, "Walk in the Spirit, and you shall not fulfill the lust of the flesh" (Galatians 5:16). How does self-control contribute to our spiritual maturity as we walk with the Lord? Why must we walk in the Spirit first in order to resist the lusts of the flesh?

4. How do the previous qualities and practices mentioned by Peter—diligence, virtue, and knowledge—help us practice self-control?

5. On a daily basis, how difficult is it for you to practice self-control? What habits or strategies help you focus on pleasing God and living by His standards?

6. Of the five discipline-building steps mentioned in the teaching, which do you currently practice? Which steps could you practice more consistently?

RESPOND

As your group concludes this third session, review the outline for the video teaching and look over any notes you took. In the space below, write down what stirred you the most from the session—whether it is from the teaching, the discussion time, your own personal study, or even a response from a group member. Consider why self-control is such a key quality for a believer in Christ to possess and how you demonstrate the quality in your own life.

PRAY

Conclude your time by sharing any personal prayer requests, and then pray for those requests as a group. Praise God for equipping you and providing you with everything you need for the tasks He has assigned to you. Ask Him to strengthen you to resist the snares of the enemy and focus on living a life of discipline and self-control in obedience to His Word.

BETWEEN-SESSIONS PERSONAL STUDY

Reflect on the material you have covered this week by engaging in any or all of the following between-session activities. Each of the questions in this section is designed to help you explore the character trait of *self-control* as you seek to *know the truth*, *unpack* the truth, and *walk* in that truth. View this time with God like a hiker views an energy bar on a long trail—as a time of refreshment and nourishment for your soul. Once again, write down your thoughts or key takeaways, as there will be time for you to share any thoughts at the next session.

KNOW THE TRUTH

The Bible reveals that Simon Peter, the author of the passage that we have been studying, was a colorful character who had quite a few rough edges. He was a fisherman by trade before he decided to follow Jesus . . . and the picture we see of Peter in the Gospels is often as stormy as the seas he sailed. Yet Peter's behavior illustrates our own personal struggles as we seek to obey God—and falter at times. Just consider this well-known scene of one of Peter's most remarkable acts of obedience:

Immediately Jesus made His disciples get into the boat and go before Him to the other side, while He sent the multitudes away. And when He had sent the multitudes away, He went up on the mountain by Himself to pray. Now when evening came, He was alone there. But the boat was now in the middle of the sea, tossed by the waves, for the wind was contrary.

Now in the fourth watch of the night Jesus went to them, walking on the sea. And when the disciples saw Him walking on the sea, they were troubled, saying, "It is a ghost!" And they cried out for fear.

But immediately Jesus spoke to them, saying, "Be of good cheer! It is I; do not be afraid."

And Peter answered Him and said, "Lord, if it is You, command me to come to You on the water."

So He said, "Come." And when Peter had come down out of the boat, he walked on the water to go to Jesus. But when he saw that the wind was boisterous, he was afraid; and beginning to sink he cried out, saying, "Lord, save me!"

And immediately Jesus stretched out His hand and caught him, and said to him, "O you of little faith, why did you doubt?" And when they got into the boat, the wind ceased.

Then those who were in the boat came and worshiped Him, saying, "Truly You are the Son of God."

MATTHEW 14:22–33

➢ When has fear caused you to lose self-control? Why is it difficult to "stay the course" and trust God when, like Peter, you are in the midst of life's storms?

➢ How does obeying God and following Christ's example empower you to "walk on water"—to do what seems impossible? When have you experienced this kind of power? What role did self-control play in seeing God work in your life?

UNPACK THE TRUTH

It's not only a matter of focusing on Christ instead of our own fears that strengthens our self-control. Throughout the Bible, the authors frequently link the concept of self-control to the Holy Spirit's work in believers' lives. In fact, this theme dominates the last half of Paul's letter to the Galatians, which can be summed up in this declaration: "I say then: Walk in the Spirit, and you shall not fulfill the lust of the flesh" (Galatians 5:16).

It may seem obvious, but the order here is vitally important. Notice that Paul does not say, "Don't fulfill the lust of the flesh, and you will walk in the Spirit." No, it's the other way around! When we are filled with the Holy Spirit each day and are completely under His control, *then* He will empower us to say no to the lusts of the flesh.

Paul goes on to list various pursuits of the flesh (see Galatians 5:19–21) before contrasting these with the fruit of the Spirit—including *self-control*: "But the fruit of the Spirit is . . . self-control. . . . And those who are Christ's have crucified the flesh with its passions and desires. If we live in the Spirit, let us also walk in the Spirit" (Galatians 5:22–25). Walking in the Spirit, particularly in regard to areas of personal weakness, requires us to surrender our struggles and ask for God's power in resisting temptation and staying the course.

Spend a few moments assessing your life in regard to your own personal discipline and how you exercise self-control. Here are a few questions to help you in this assessment.

➤ When is a time you realized you were relying on your own strength in attempting to overcome a temptation or maintain self-control? What made you come to this realization?

➤ When is a time you relied on God's power to sustain you and strengthen your self-discipline? What differences do you notice between the two approaches—particularly as it relates to your mindset, attitude, and behavior?

➤ What are your areas of greatest struggle as you practice self-control? As you have prayed this week, what strategies have you found for leaning into God's strength to face these struggles?

> ➤ Who has helped you practice self-control—either by their example, counsel, encouragement—in pursuing a godly life? How did their input assist you in relying on God for your self-control?

WALK IN TRUTH

One of the greatest barriers to our self-control is often *busyness*—in particular, our dependence on technology and social media. It is not necessarily that being plugged in makes us weaker, though it certainly presents more opportunities for temptation, but it is more a matter of how our electronic devices consume our time and attention. We forget how to still our heart before God and seek time alone with Him. His voice gets lost in the noise of so many voices, sound bites, and podcasts.

Before the next time your group meets, set aside at least one hour—two, if possible—to unplug from the world. Remove as many distractions as possible, such as work or family responsibilities, and spend the time focused on God and the priorities you have for your relationship with Him. You may want to spend your time with Him outdoors in His creation or spend part of the time reading and studying His Word. The emphasis is simply on re-centering your heart on your first love and letting the Holy Spirit speak to you.

FOR NEXT WEEK

If you are reading *Everything You Need* as you complete this study, read chapter 6, "Relentless Determination," in preparation for next week. Use the space below to write any key insights or questions from your personal study that you want to discuss at the next group meeting.

PERSEVERE ON THE PATH

Perseverance is a never-give-up attitude, a commitment to move forward when everything is conspiring to hold you back. Perseverance turns ordeals into opportunities. It gives us the opportunity to finish what we begin, to outlast pain and sorrow, to strive until we accomplish things that are difficult, and to demonstrate God's grace in all the seasons of life. Those who learn to persevere are forces to be reckoned with. In a world where most people give up and give out, those who keep going will accomplish more than they know.

DR. DAVID JEREMIAH

WELCOME

Whenever you set out to achieve a goal, you can be certain that you will encounter obstacles along the way that will threaten to hinder your progress. Unplanned detours will spring up that will force to you find a different route to move forward. Problems and setbacks will suddenly arise that will hinder your forward momentum. Difficulties and crises will roll in like unexpected thunderstorms off the plains . . . leaving you feeling confused, drenched, and overwhelmed.

Often, the trail of life will seem to become steeper just as you grow more winded from the exertion you had to expend to even get that far. The friction you experience in your day will cause "blisters" and "scrapes" that make it painful to take the next step on your journey. At times you may also lose sight of the summit—the view you had from the start that had continuously provided the incentive for you to complete your trek. You might wonder if you are ever going to reach your destination—and if you do, whether the journey will be worth it.

While it may be difficult to accept, your spiritual journey will also have its share of unexpected obstacles, distracting detours, and dangerous storms. As Jesus said, "In the world you will have tribulation" (John 16:33). The Word of God promises that you will encounter setbacks and obstacles as you traverse through life. What matters is your response. The way that you react and handle those challenges makes all the difference in the world.

As we have seen in the key passage we have been studying, God has given us the qualities of virtue, knowledge, and self-control to assist us on our journey to a life of godliness. But as we will discover in this week's study, the Lord has provided us with another key resource that will help us to get through those stormy times when we feel we are trudging through a dark valley. As Peter explains, this resource is *perseverance* (see 2 Peter 1:6).

SHARE

Take a few minutes at the start of this session to go around the group and share any insights you have from last week's personal study. Then discuss one of the following questions:

- When have you been traveling and encountered an obstacle that forced you to change your route? How did you feel about having to take a new path?

— *or* —

- What are some of the situations you face in life that require you to persevere? What have you learned from those experiences?

READ

Invite someone in the group to read the following passage as everyone listens. Then turn to the person on your right and answer the questions that follow.

> Therefore we also, since we are surrounded by so great a cloud of witnesses, let us lay aside every weight, and the sin which so easily ensnares us, and let us run with endurance the race that is set before us, looking unto Jesus, the author and finisher of our faith, who for the joy that was set before Him endured the cross, despising the shame, and has sat down at the right hand of the throne of God. For consider Him who endured such hostility from sinners against Himself, lest you become weary and discouraged in your souls.
>
> HEBREWS 12:1–3

➢ According to the author of Hebrews, what keeps us from becoming "weary and discouraged in [our] souls" as we "run with endurance the race that is set before us"?

➤ What usually motivates you to finish something you've started—particularly as it relates to a big project or a long-term goal?

WATCH

Play the video for session four. As you watch, use the following notes to record any thoughts, questions, or key points that stand out to you.

NOTES

Perseverance is a never-give-up attitude—a commitment to move forward when everything is conspiring to hold you back. When you persevere, you find ways to look beyond your ordeals and find opportunities—for growth, advancement, and productivity.

There are several biblical strategies that can help us persevere through difficult times. The first is to *put our problems into perspective* by considering them in light of eternity.

The second strategy is to *learn to tackle just today*. We don't have to solve every problem, overcome every obstacle, or accomplish our entire journey all at once.

The third strategy is to *surround ourselves with encouragers* who will support us, pray for us, cheer us on, comfort us, and help keep us going.

The fourth strategy is to *know when to rest*. God rested after creating the world, and Jesus took time to rest during His mission. We need to follow this example.

The fifth strategy is to *cultivate a positive attitude*. We can choose to be defined by the reality of Christ within us and the peace that He has provided.

The final strategy is to *refuse to quit*. God rewards our commitment to push through problems. We must trust that He will work through us to complete this stretch of our journey.

When we keep our eyes on Jesus, He gives us the ability to persevere through challenges, the stamina to confront problems, and the strength to never grow weary or lose heart.

DISCUSS

Take a few minutes with your group members to discuss what you just watched and explore these concepts in Scripture. Use the following questions to help guide your discussion.

1. What is your definition of *perseverance*? What has motivated you to keep going through life's greatest challenges?

2. How does knowledge of God's Word help you to keep the proper perspective on your problems? How does maintaining an active prayer life help you see your difficulties from God's perspective and keep moving forward?

3. Jesus said, "Do not worry about tomorrow, for tomorrow will worry about its own things" (Matthew 6:34). What are some ways you have found that help you focus only on today's problems and not worry about the ones that may come tomorrow?

4. Who are some encouragers in your life? How do they help you persevere?

5. How has Christ's example of knowing when to rest, maintaining a positive attitude, and refusing to quit helped you persevere?

RESPOND

As your group concludes this fourth session, review the outline for the video teaching and look over any notes you took. In the space below, write down one or two of your main takeaways from this session. Consider what role perseverance plays in your life and which of the strategies discussed in the teaching are ones you need to continue to develop.

PRAY

Conclude your time by sharing any personal prayer requests—including any burdens you are facing that are stretching your ability to persevere. Lift up one another's requests, asking God to give you His strength, stamina, and peace as you keep your eyes fixed on Jesus and run the race that has been set for you. Thank God that He provides everything you need to keep going.

BETWEEN-SESSIONS PERSONAL STUDY

Reflect on the material you have covered this week by engaging in any or all of the following between-session activities. Each of the questions in this section is designed to help you explore the character trait of *perseverance* as you seek to *know* the truth, *unpack* the truth, and *walk* in that truth. Keep the other attributes we have covered in this study—diligence, virtue, knowledge, and self-control—in mind as you do these exercises and consider how your ability to persevere relates to each of them. Continue to write down your thoughts or key takeaways, as there will be time for you to share any thoughts at the next session.

KNOW THE TRUTH

If anyone knew about encountering obstacles and enduring trials, it was the apostle Paul. He faced just about every possible setback imaginable. Persecution from religious and political leaders. An arrest, conviction, and jail time for preaching the gospel. Stormy sea voyages and shipwrecks. Snakebites and earthquakes . . .

and more. However, no matter what Paul was facing, he knew he could rely on God as the source of his strength and the basis for his contentment. Notice in the passage below how Paul remained honest about his struggles in the moment but looked to Jesus in order to press forward and persevere:

> But we have this treasure in earthen vessels, that the excellence of the power may be of God and not of us. We are hard-pressed on every side, yet not crushed; we are perplexed, but not in despair; persecuted, but not forsaken; struck down, but not destroyed—always carrying about in the body the dying of the Lord Jesus, that the life of Jesus also may be manifested in our body. For we who live are always delivered to death for Jesus' sake, that the life of Jesus also may be manifested in our mortal flesh. So then death is working in us, but life in you.
>
> And since we have the same spirit of faith, according to what is written, "I believed and therefore I spoke," we also believe and therefore speak, knowing that He who raised up the Lord Jesus will also raise us up with Jesus, and will present us with you. For all things are for your sakes, that grace, having spread through the many, may cause thanksgiving to abound to the glory of God.
>
> 2 CORINTHIANS 4:7–15

➢ How did Paul remain positive and rely on his faith without denying the hardships he was facing? How does he express a balanced view and maintain an eternal perspective?

➤ What does it mean for you to have eternal treasure in your "earthen vessel"? How does focusing on eternal spiritual realities help you face the physical struggles of everyday life?

UNPACK THE TRUTH

Perseverance results in the transformation of our character because as we press forward, we learn much along the way. In fact, the Bible teaches that perseverance is at the *heart* of maturity. As Paul concludes, "We know that suffering produces perseverance; perseverance, character; and character, hope" (Romans 5:3–4 NIV). James echoes this truth when he writes, "Consider it pure joy, my brothers and sisters, whenever you face trials of many kinds, because you know that the testing of your faith produces perseverance. Let perseverance finish its work so that you may be mature and complete, not lacking anything" (James 1:2–4 NIV).

As we see in both passages, *perseverance is the essence of maturity.* If we cannot persevere, then we will not mature. God allows us to face trials in this life because He knows it will lead us to trust in Him and press on with grit and grace—the very definition of perseverance. This is what exercising faith in our race of endurance is all about. As Paul writes:

Do you not know that those who run in a race all run, but one receives the prize? Run in such a way that you may obtain it. And everyone who competes for the prize is temperate in all things. Now they do it to obtain a perishable crown, but we for an imperishable crown. Therefore I run thus: not with uncertainty. Thus I fight: not as one who beats the air. But I discipline my body and bring it into subjection, lest, when I have preached to others, I myself should become disqualified.

1 CORINTHIANS 9:24–27

Spiritual transformation doesn't just *happen*—it's forged through the fire of difficulty. When we maintain our trust in God in spite difficulty or disaster, it produces a strength of conviction, ethics, courage, and resilience that becomes part of our character. With this process in mind, think back over the major struggles in your life. What have you learned along the way? What has God revealed to you through those battles? In the space below, describe at least three of these "active learning" situations and the wisdom gleaned from each one.

Trial or struggle #1:

Lessons learned and wisdom gained:

Trial or struggle #2:

Lessons learned and wisdom gained:

Trial or struggle #3:

Lessons learned and wisdom gained:

WALK IN TRUTH

Avid hikers know how daunting it can be to look at the distance required to get from their starting point to their destination. With added challenges caused by variables such as weather or trail conditions, these experienced hikers know that after they have planned and prepared for their journey, they must simply begin. Putting one foot in front of the other, they move toward their destination step by step, moment by moment, hour by hour.

In order to persevere in the faith, we must do the same. Our job is simply to keep putting one foot in front of the other—to tackle each day step by step. In the Bible, we read that when God appointed Joshua as leader of the Israelites and gave him the responsibility for leading the Israelites through the Jordan River and into the Promised Land, He told him, "I will give you every place where you set your foot" (Joshua 1:3 NIV). Like Joshua, we cannot make progress unless we go forward one step at a time—knowing each step will be a victory.

We don't have to conquer all our problems at once, nor do we need to accomplish our life's work in one day. God's plan is step by step, moment by moment, day by day. Remember what Jesus said in the Sermon on the Mount: "Therefore I say to you, do not worry about your life, what you will eat or what you will drink; nor about your body, what you will put on. Is not life more than food and the body more than clothing? . . . But seek first the kingdom of God and His righteousness, and all these things shall be added to you" (Matthew 6:25, 33).

Today, choose one struggle, conflict, problem, or obstacle that is currently looming in front of you. As you consider this issue—accepting that you cannot solve it, fix it, deny it, or delete it—think of one step (*just one*) that you can take right now to move forward. Write down your "marching orders" in the space below and how taking this step will make you feel.

Now spend a few moments in prayer, asking God to empower you to take this one step as you trust Him for everything you need. Then, with His help . . . just do it!

FOR NEXT WEEK

If you are reading *Everything You Need* as you complete this study, read chapter 7, "Christlike Character," and chapter 8, "Radical Kindness," in preparation for next week. Use the space below to write any key insights or questions from your personal study that you want to discuss at the next group meeting.

STEP OUT TO HELP

In a sense, we're all like postal carriers assigned our individual routes on this planet. You're a special delivery messenger with a letter from heaven—the Bible—and with the words of the good news of Christ, postmarked with the blood of Calvary. Your zip code is wherever God sends you day by day. By the time you finish your task, your message will touch thousands of people—maybe millions. Never let snow or rain nor heat nor gloom of night hinder you. Instead, be first class in your actions and attitudes. Seal your work with brotherly kindness, and God will stamp your life with His blessing.

DR. DAVID JEREMIAH

WELCOME

Traveling alone tends not to be very enjoyable. Sure, you get to make all the decisions as to where you will go and what you will see . . . but you are also left with the reality that you have no one with whom to share your experiences along the way. And if you happen to sustain an injury, run out of resources, or lose your way while on your own, you have no one else to rely on for help. Even if everything goes smoothly, you may still feel lonely and disconnected by the lack of company.

Walking by faith is also more difficult when you try to do it by yourself. The Bible is clear that God never intended for any of us to take this journey of faith alone. He has placed people in your path so you can have fellowship and gain strength from them when the way grows difficult. In the same vein, He has also placed people in your life so you can extend kindness to them, encourage them, and support them in their journey. As you do this, you take yet another step toward your goal of leading a godly life—and becoming more like Christ.

Throughout this study, we have seen how God has given us everything we need to grow in godliness. Remember, as Peter writes, "His divine power has given to us *all things* that pertain to life and godliness, through the knowledge of Him who called us by glory and virtue" (2 Peter 1:3, emphasis added). As we develop the traits we have discussed—virtue, knowledge, self-control, and perseverance—we grow in our faith and become more like Christ.

Yet while God helps us develop these traits as individuals, our Christian journey is designed to be a team endeavor, not a solitary expedition. The Bible tells us to "consider one another in order to stir up love and good works, not forsaking the assembling of ourselves together, as is the manner of some, but exhorting one another" (Hebrews 10:24–25). So it is no wonder the next two items on Peter's list are more outward-focused. He states that we are to add "to perseverance godliness, to godliness brotherly kindness" (2 Peter 1:6–7).

SHARE

Take a few minutes at the start of this session to go around the group and share any insights you have from last week's personal study. Then discuss one of the following questions:

- When was the last time you traveled alone? What do you like about being by yourself? What is more challenging when you don't have others with you?

— or —

- What are some tangible ways you have recently experienced the kindness of others? What impact did their actions have on you?

READ

Invite someone in the group to read the following passage as everyone listens. Then turn to the person nearest you and answer the questions that follow.

I, therefore, the prisoner of the Lord, beseech you to walk worthy of the calling with which you were called, with all lowliness and gentleness, with longsuffering, bearing with one another in love, endeavoring to keep the unity of the Spirit in the bond of peace. There is one body and one Spirit, just as you were called in one hope of your calling; one Lord, one faith, one baptism; one God and Father of all, who is above all, and through all, and in you all. . . .

Therefore, putting away lying, "Let each one of you speak truth with his neighbor," for we are members of one another. "Be angry, and do not sin": do not let the sun go down on your wrath, nor give place to the devil. Let him who stole steal no longer, but rather let him labor, working with his hands what is good, that he may have something to give him who has need. Let no corrupt word proceed out of your mouth, but what is good for necessary edification, that it may impart grace to the hearers. And do not grieve the Holy Spirit of God, by whom you were sealed for the day of redemption. Let all bitterness, wrath, anger, clamor, and evil speaking be put away from you, with all malice. And be kind to one another, tenderhearted, forgiving one another, even as God in Christ forgave you.

Ephesians 4:1–6, 25–32

➤ What does it mean to "walk worthy of the calling with which you were called"? What impact does walking worthy have on our relationships?

➤ Why is our code of conduct as Christ-followers different from others in the world? What makes us—and our standard—different?

WATCH

Play the video for session five. As you watch, use the following notes to record any thoughts, questions, or key points that stand out to you.

NOTES

Followers of Christ are called to lead godly lives, which includes reflecting Jesus' qualities in our relationships with others.

Godliness requires us to *examine our identity in Christ*. Regardless of our family background, past mistakes, or current season in life, we are all valuable in God's eyes. We belong to Him.

We are also *pilgrims on a journey with Christ*. As citizens of heaven, earth is not our home. We are just passing through in our mortal bodies in pursuit of our eternal destination.

We are God's *platform in this world*—His pulpit for proclaiming the life-saving message of Christ. God chose us to serve as His ambassadors as part of a body known as the church.

When we realize we are God's platform, it compels us to *carry out our assignment in His kingdom.* As we reflect the traits of godliness in our life and as we practice radical kindness, we draw those in the outside world to Christ.

In Ephesians 4:25–32, Paul provides us with seven truths that instruct and illustrate the way we should interact with others:

- We forge our friendships with trust

- We free our relationships from anger

- We feed the hungry

- We fortify others with our words

- We release bitterness from our spirit

- We find new ways to practice kindness

- We forgive others as Christ forgave us

We can truly make an eternal difference in the lives of others when we offer them "a cup of cold water"—showing them love, care, and mercy—in the name of Christ.

DISCUSS

Take a few minutes with your group members to discuss what you just watched and explore these concepts in Scripture. Use the following questions to help guide your discussion.

1. Peter states that believers are "a chosen generation, a royal priesthood, a holy nation, His own special people" (1 Peter 2:9). What does it mean to be one of God's "own special people"? What does this reveal about the way God sees your worth?

2. Why is it so important to remember that heaven—not earth—is your home and your ultimate destination? How does this truth motivate you to lead a godly life?

3. How does knowing that you serve as God's ambassador influence your decisions on a daily basis? How should this truth affect your thoughts, words, actions, and habits?

4. God calls His children to forge their friendships with truth and free their relationships from anger. Why do you think He stresses this point? In what ways have you found this challenging to do in all of your relationships?

5. How are you fortifying others with your words? Do others see godliness reflected in your texts, chats, comments, tweets, blogs, and emails as well as your words and actions in person? Why or why not?

6. Who has crossed your path recently with whom you feel drawn to share God's love? How have you shown them who God is through your interactions?

RESPOND

As your group concludes this fifth session, pause for a moment to reflect on what stands out to you from the teaching. What part do relationships play in your journey through life? How has God given you everything you need to love those in your world? What can you do today to extend brotherly kindness to another person in your life? Write down your thoughts below.

PRAY

Conclude your time together by going around the group and allowing each person to share his or her needs and requests. Then spend a few moments in silence before praying for one another. In addition to your requests, thank God for the people He has placed in your life right now. Invite Him to use you to reflect His character and grace to everyone you know.

BETWEEN-SESSIONS PERSONAL STUDY

Reflect on the material you have covered this week by engaging in any or all of the following between-session activities. Each of the questions in this section is designed to help you explore the character traits of *godliness* and *radical kindness* as you seek to *know* the truth, *unpack* the truth, and *walk* in that truth. As you work through this study, think about your relationships and how your interactions with others has helped you to both increase in godliness and also shine Christ's love into their lives. Write down your thoughts or key takeaways, as there will be time for you to share any thoughts at the next session.

KNOW THE TRUTH

Our spiritual transformation begins when we receive Jesus as our Savior. We are forgiven, made pure in God's sight, and given eternal life. Yet we are not yet perfected like Christ. Some changes may happen immediately, but growing in God's holiness is a life-long endeavor—and we must do our part in the process. As we consistently choose to think, speak, act, and serve like Jesus, we grow in Him and become increasingly more like Him. Peter described this process in his first letter by contrasting who we used to be with who we are currently in Christ:

> But you are a chosen generation, a royal priesthood, a holy nation, His own special people, that you may proclaim the praises of Him who called you out of darkness into His marvelous light; who once were not a people but are now the people of God, who had not obtained mercy but now have obtained mercy. Beloved, I beg you as sojourners and pilgrims, abstain from fleshly lusts which war against the soul, having your conduct honorable among the Gentiles, that when they speak against you as evildoers, they may, by your good works which they observe, glorify God in the day of visitation.
>
> *1 PETER 2:9–12*

➤ How does Peter describe your life prior to accepting Jesus? After you have Christ in your life? What words does Peter use to illustrate this before-and-after comparison?

> ➤ What do others see in your life right now that glorifies God?
>   What words, actions, and habits do others see that you need
>   to adjust to better reflect true godliness?

UNPACK THE TRUTH

As we have explored throughout this study, God has given us everything we need to lead a godly life through His precious promises. Yet in addition to diligence, virtue, knowledge, self-control, perseverance, and godliness, Peter also emphasizes that we need "brotherly kindness" (2 Peter 1:7). The word that Peter uses in the original Greek was one familiar to most people: *philadelphia*. We know the term because William Penn, the founder of Pennsylvania, wanted to establish a city characterized by this very biblical trait.

Of course, practicing this form of kindness is vital not only for residents of Philadelphia but also for all who wish to follow Christ. Furthermore, Peter was not the only person in the Bible to emphasize this quality. In Ephesians 4:25–32, the apostle Paul lists seven practices that are just as relevant to us today if we are serious about living godly lives that reflect divine kindness. We considered these practices during the group time this week, but now consider them on a more personal level. As you think through your answers to the questions below, allow the Holy Spirit to reveal areas that need more attention, effort, and practice.

> *Forge your friendships with trust:* How willing are you to trust your friends and loved ones? What is your basis for trusting them? How do you actively build trust with others?

> *Free your relationships from anger:* When was the last time you expressed your anger at someone? What steps did you take to resolve the conflict with that person?

> *Feed the hungry:* On average, how often do you serve others in some notable way? Do you serve to be recognized or to show God's generosity to those in need? Explain.

➤ *Fortify others with your words:* Have you encouraged someone with your words today? What did you tell them? Can you think of another individual who would benefit from your words of encouragement on a regular basis?

➤ *Flush bitterness from your spirit:* Do you regularly stop and reflect on those conversations, events, and people who annoy you, frustrate you, or anger you? How many are you hanging on to right now? What do you need to release in order to flush out bitterness from your spirit?

➤ *Find new ways to practice kindness:* When was the last time you acted on an opportunity to demonstrate kindness to a stranger? To your famlly, friends, coworkers, or neighbors? How can you make looking for such opportunities more of a daily practice?

➤ *Forgive as Christ forgave you:* Who has hurt you, offended you, or harmed you that you need to forgive? Whom have you hurt, offended, or harmed and need to ask forgiveness from?

WALK IN TRUTH

We are called to lead godly lives in all areas, but perhaps our relationships reflect our godliness—or lack of it—better than any other area. God created us to be social beings who long for intimacy and community with one another, but we often struggle to treat others the way we want to be treated. And no matter how godly we are, we can always do more to show others the love of Christ and the grace of God that has transformed our life.

Before your next group session, choose at least one specific practice from the seven listed in the "Unpack the Truth" section above and make a plan for how you will implement it. For instance, you might need to meet with a friend and apologize for something you have said or done that hurt this person. Asking for forgiveness is humbling, but it reflects the grace and mercy of God that you have received in your own life.

Or, you might feel led to serve someone in your church, neighborhood, or community. You might see a need that you can meet—perhaps anonymously. Or maybe you just need to spend some time alone with God and confess the bitterness and resentment that you have allowed to fester inside of you. Whatever practice you choose, ask God to work through you so that others may see Him more clearly.

FOR NEXT WEEK

If you are reading *Everything You Need* as you complete this study, read chapter 9, "Selfless Love," and chapter 10, "The Blessing," in preparation for next week. Use the space below to write any key insights or questions from your personal study that you want to discuss at the next group meeting.

REACH THE DESTINATION

One by one, like dominos toppling each other, we've come closer to the final supreme quality of Christlikeness: love. Love is the final quality on Peter's list because it's the most important. It completes and gives meaning to the rest. Even if you cultivate all of the character qualities we've explored in this book and mastered them, they would be meaningless if they weren't saturated with love. Love is your deepest need and your highest blessing.

DR. DAVID JEREMIAH

WELCOME

It is exhilarating to finally reach a destination that you have been pursuing and working to reach. Whether it took hours, days, or even weeks, the journey suddenly seems worthwhile as you enjoy the sense of accomplishment that comes from achieving a goal. There may also be a sense of personal satisfaction in knowing you were able to not only persevere but also help others along the way. Little in life is more fulfilling than knowing that because of your kindness, others are able to enjoy the same sense of achievement.

While your ultimate heavenly destination is still ahead of you, your journey of faith also provides some exciting milestones along the way. There is something stimulating in knowing that in spite of the obstacles, setbacks, and temporary struggles you endured, your perseverance—and reliance on God's resources—has enabled you to reach your destination. For the believer in Christ, that destination can be summed up by Peter's instruction to add "to godliness brotherly kindness, and to brotherly kindness *love*" (2 Peter 1:7, emphasis added).

Just as God has put people in your life who will show you love and encouragement, He has put you into other people's lives so you can show them love and encouragement. Jesus proclaimed that the greatest commandment was to "love the LORD your God with all your heart" and that the second was like it: "love your neighbor as yourself" (Matthew 22:37–39). The type of love to which Jesus was referring was not a simple exchange of pleasantries or even feelings of affection. Rather, He was speaking of a *self-sacrificing* love—a love that motivates you to give everything to God and others. Jesus calls you to give your all to others—including the difficult ones—and put their needs above your own.

One by one, we have passed all the milestones on the trail and come to this final quality. All of the character traits we have discussed have been building on each other to reach this ultimate destination. And as you rely on *all* the tools God has provided for you—diligence, virtue, knowledge, self-control, perseverance, godliness, brotherly kindness, and love—they will guide you forward and lead you into the abundant life He has planned for you.

SHARE

Take a few minutes at the start of this session to go around the group and share any insights you have from last week's personal study. Then discuss one of the following questions:

- How do you respond to the idea of *self-sacrificing love* being the "destination" for a believer in Christ? Why is reaching this place a lifelong endeavor?

— or —

- As you consider each of the qualities that we have discussed during this study, which is currently the most challenging for you? At what point in the "journey" would you say that you are right now?

READ

Invite someone in the group to read the following passage as everyone listens. Then pair up with someone sitting near you and answer the questions that follow.

Now before the Feast of the Passover, when Jesus knew that His hour had come that He should depart from this world to the Father, having loved His own who were in the world, He loved them to the end.

And supper being ended, the devil having already put it into the heart of Judas Iscariot, Simon's son, to betray Him, Jesus, knowing that the Father had given all things into His hands, and that He had come from God and was going to God, rose from supper and laid aside His garments, took a towel and girded Himself. After that, He poured water into a basin and began to wash the disciples' feet, and to wipe them with the towel with which He was girded. . . .

So when He had washed their feet, taken His garments, and sat down again, He said to them, "Do you know what I have done to you? You call Me Teacher and Lord, and you say well, for so I am. If I then, your Lord and Teacher, have washed your feet, you also ought to wash one another's feet. For I have given you an example, that you should do as I have done to you. Most assuredly, I say to you, a servant is not greater than his master; nor is he who is sent greater than he who sent him. If you know these things, blessed are you if you do them."

JOHN 13:1–5, 12–17

➤ Why is it significant that Jesus even washed the feet of Judas Iscariot—the one who would soon betray Him? What does this say about the types of people whom He expects us to love?

➤ What act of service has someone done for you lately that demonstrated their love? Or what have you done to demonstrate your love to someone else?

WATCH

Play the video for session six. As you watch, use the following notes to record any thoughts, questions, or key points that stand out to you.

NOTES

Love is the final quality on Peter's list because it is the most important trait that we can possess. Love completes and gives meaning to all the rest.

The humble act of service that Jesus performs in John 13 by washing His disciples' feet reveals five insights on how we can lovingly serve others today. First, *love helps us navigate our lifelong journey.* When the time came for Jesus to die, He gathered with His disciples in an upper room one last time to celebrate Passover. His love for them endured to the end.

Second, *love motivates us to serve others.* If Jesus was willing to humble Himself and wash the feet of His disciples—including Judas—then we can love others with the same humility.

Third, *love imitates the Lord Jesus.* After washing the disciples' feet, Jesus commanded His disciples to follow His example of sacrificial love. His command still applies to us today.

Fourth, *love elevates the experience of life.* We cannot share the love of Jesus without being blessed in the process. Every time the current of Jesus' love flows through us, we experience the joy, satisfaction, and blessings that come from being a conduit of godly love.

Finally, *love authenticates our discipleship.* We are called to love others in the same way Jesus loved us (see 1 John 3:16). When we give everything that we can to love others, the world notices.

Peter ends his message to us by providing a list of seven blessings that flow into our life when we put these teachings into practice:

- Godly maturity

- Growing productivity

- Greater clarity

- Grateful memory

- Genuine stability

- Guaranteed security

• Glorious eternity

Jesus gave everything He had so we could have everything we need to lead the life God wants us to live. No matter what obstacles lie ahead, the qualities we need to navigate every difficulty, distraction, and delay are available to us in abundance.

DISCUSS

Take a few minutes with your group members to discuss what you just watched and explore these concepts in Scripture. Use the following questions to help guide your discussion.

1. Why is love so important in exercising the other attributes Peter has listed?

2. How did Jesus' love for His disciples enhance the three years He spent with them? How was this symbolized by Jesus' act of washing their feet?

3. How does Jesus' example of sacrificial love—both in washing His disciples' feet and dying on the cross for your sins— motivate you to serve others?

4. With Jesus as your role model, what are some ways you are sacrificially loving and servings others right now?

5. How has serving humbly and sacrificially like Christ enhanced your life experiences? What has it cost you to serve this way?

6. Which of Peter's seven blessings (listed in 2 Peter 1:8–11) resonates with you the most? Why does this particular blessing resonate with you?

RESPOND

As your group concludes this final session, review the outline for the video teaching and look over any notes you took. Think back over your group meetings and consider how God has truly provided *everything you need* to lead a life of faith and godliness. Think of one key takeaway from the entire study and record it in the space below.

PRAY

Conclude your time by sharing any personal prayer requests, and then pray for those requests as a group. Thank God and praise Him for everything you have learned and experienced together during the course of this group study. Ask the Lord to continue empowering and equipping each of you as you continue on your journey. Seek His blessings, including the seven listed by Peter in this session, as you put what you've learned into practice by loving others.

FINAL PERSONAL STUDY

Reflect on the material you have covered during this final week by engaging in any or all of the following activities. Each of the questions in this section is designed to help you explore the final character trait of *selfless love* and experience God's blessing as you seek to *know* the truth, *unpack* the truth, and *walk* in that truth. As you work through this study, consider how God has used your group to empower and equip you for the next leg of your journey. Ask Him to guide you as you complete the following questions and exercises, illuminating any areas that need clarity and providing direction for your next steps.

KNOW THE TRUTH

Everything in this study is summed up by the biblical word *agape*—the heavenly brand of love that is ours in Jesus. *Agape* is a self-sacrificing love that motivates us to give our all for God and others. Sometimes giving our all may cost us our very life . . .

but on most days it means we live out our commitment to God and others, serving with selfless devotion.

Through Jesus, God has given us the greatest love there is. His Word tells us, "The love of God has been poured out in our hearts by the Holy Spirit who was given to us" (Romans 5:5). As the apostle Paul explains, love is what matters the most:

> Though I speak with the tongues of men and of angels, but have not love, I have become sounding brass or a clanging cymbal. And though I have the gift of prophecy, and understand all mysteries and all knowledge, and though I have all faith, so that I could remove mountains, but have not love, I am nothing. And though I bestow all my goods to feed the poor, and though I give my body to be burned, but have not love, it profits me nothing.
>
> Love suffers long and is kind; love does not envy; love does not parade itself, is not puffed up; does not behave rudely, does not seek its own, is not provoked, thinks no evil; does not rejoice in iniquity, but rejoices in the truth; bears all things, believes all things, hopes all things, endures all things.
>
> Love never fails. But whether there are prophecies, they will fail; whether there are tongues, they will cease; whether there is knowledge, it will vanish away. For we know in part and we prophesy in part. But when that which is perfect has come, then that which is in part will be done away.
>
> When I was a child, I spoke as a child, I understood as a child, I thought as a child; but when I became a man, I put away childish things. For now we see in a mirror, dimly, but then face to face. Now I know in part, but then I shall know just as I also am known.

And now abide faith, hope, love, these three; but the greatest of these is love.

1 CORINTHIANS 13:1–13

➤ How does love, as Paul described it in this passage, defy logic and human expectations? How does this kind of love make perfect sense in light of God's character and Christ's sacrifice?

➤ Looking back on your life, when have you experienced this kind of Christlike, unconditional love? When have you experienced it most recently?

UNPACK THE TRUTH

It seems only fitting that Peter ends his list of godly attributes with the most important of all: love. As if to demonstrate this quality, he then concludes by offering us seven blessings. Five are available to us now, while two await us in the future. Today, as you read the following passage, let these blessings encourage you as you recognize the truth that God has given you everything you need so He can bless you in every imaginable way!

> For if these things are yours and abound, you will be neither barren nor unfruitful in the knowledge of our Lord Jesus Christ. For he who lacks these things is shortsighted, even to blindness, and has forgotten that he was cleansed from his old sins. Therefore, brethren, be even more diligent to make your call and election sure, for if you do these things you will never stumble; for so an entrance will be supplied to you abundantly into the everlasting kingdom of our Lord and Savior Jesus Christ.
>
> 2 PETER 1:8–11

Spend a few moments reflecting on the seven blessings that Peter notes in this passage:

- *Godly maturity:* Peter wanted his readers to do more than just have faith—he wanted them to devote themselves to growing deeper, wider, and richer in their faith. God wants the same for you . . . an *abundant* faith.

- *Growing productivity:* If you possess the qualities Peter lists and grow in them, you will be effective for Christ. The key to productivity is the diligent development of godly character.

- *Greater clarity:* As you grow in the grace of Jesus, your vision becomes clear. You see His blessings and focus on things that are eternal.

- *Grateful memory:* As you grow in these qualities, you keep Jesus at the forefront of your mind, always remembering how He has rescued, restored, and blessed you.

- *Genuine stability:* As you grow in Christ, you will become more emotionally stable, spiritually sturdy, and solid in your beliefs and behaviors. You will confirm your faith by your faithfulness, which brings stability to your life.

- *Guaranteed security:* If you are actively pursuing a godly life, your progress in the faith will serve as reassurance of your salvation.

- *Glorious eternity:* If you diligently add these qualities to your life, you will be given a rich and abundant entrance into eternity.

Choose one of these blessings that especially stands out to you, and then answer the following questions.

➢ How has this study helped you to understand or experience this blessing in your life?

➢ How does thinking about this blessing you have received empower you to love more completely and sacrificially as you interact with others on a daily basis?

➢ How has your perspective on love changed since beginning this study? What has helped you to love more like Jesus?

➢ What truths has God revealed to you through this study? How has He blessed you?

WALK IN TRUTH

Spend some time in prayer and thank God for providing *everything you need* for the next part of your journey with Him. Seek the Holy Spirit's guidance as you consider if there is a Bible study, group ministry project, or church outreach you should consider joining. Contact at least one other member of your group in the upcoming week and encourage him or her on their path.

Look for opportunities to offer unexpected kindness to everyone around you—including those you may find difficult to love. Live as one who has been given a priceless treasure and who has been called to share it with the world. Remember, as you trek through life, you don't have a few things or a couple things to lead a godly life—*you have everything you need!*

LEADER'S GUIDE

Thank you for your willingness to lead your group through this study! What you have chosen to do is valuable and will make a great difference in the lives of others. The rewards of being a leader are different from those of participating, and we hope that as you lead you will find your own walk with Jesus deepened by this experience.

Everything You Need is a six-session study built around video content and small-group interaction. As the group leader, think of yourself as the host. Your job is to take care of your guests by managing the behind-the-scenes details so that when everyone arrives, they can enjoy their time together. As the leader, your role is not to answer all the questions or reteach the content—the video, book, and study guide will do that work. Your job is to guide the experience and cultivate your small group into a teaching community. This will make it a place for members to process, question, and reflect—not receive more instruction.

Before your first meeting, make sure everyone in the group gets a copy of the study guide. This will keep everyone on the same page and help the process to run more smoothly. If some group members are unable to purchase the guide, arrange it so that people can share the resource with other group members.

Giving everyone access to all the material will position this study to be as rewarding an experience as possible. Everyone should feel free to write in his or her study guide and bring it every week.

SETTING UP THE GROUP

Your group will need to determine how long you want to meet each week so you can plan your time accordingly. Generally, most groups like to meet for either sixty minutes or ninety minutes, so you could use one of the following schedules:

SECTION	60 MINUTES	90 MINUTES
Welcome (members arrive and get settled)	5 minutes	5 minutes
Share (discuss one of the opening questions for the session)	5 minutes	10 minutes
Read (discuss the questions based on the Scripture reading for the session)	5 minutes	10 minutes
Watch (watch the video teaching material together and take notes)	15 minutes	15 minutes
Discuss (discuss the Bible study questions based on the video teaching)	25 minutes	40 minutes
Respond/Pray (reflect on the key insights, pray together, and dismiss)	5 minutes	10 minutes

As the group leader, you will want to create an environment that encourages sharing and learning. A church sanctuary or formal classroom may not be as ideal as a living room, because those locations can feel formal and less intimate. No matter what setting you choose, provide enough comfortable seating for everyone, and, if possible, arrange the seats in a semicircle so everyone can see the video easily. This will make the transition between the video and group conversation more efficient and natural.

Also, try to get to the meeting site early so you can greet participants as they arrive. Simple refreshments create a welcoming atmosphere and can be a wonderful addition to a group study. Try to take food and pet allergies into account to make your guests as comfortable as possible. You may also want to consider offering childcare to couples with children who want to attend. Finally, be sure your media technology is working properly. Managing these details up front will make the rest of your group experience flow smoothly and provide a welcoming space in which to engage with the content of *Everything You Need*.

STARTING THE GROUP TIME

Once everyone has arrived, it is time to begin the study. Here are some simple tips to make your group time healthy, enjoyable, and effective.

Begin the meeting with a short prayer and remind the group members to put their phones on silent. This is a way to make sure you can all be present with one another and with God. Next, give each person a few minutes to respond to the questions in the

"Share" and "Read" sections. This won't require as much time in session one, but beginning in session two, people will need more time to share their insights from their personal studies. Usually, you won't answer the discussion questions yourself, but you should go first with the "Share" and "Read" questions, answering briefly and with a reasonable amount of transparency.

At the end of session one, invite the group members to complete the "Between-Sessions Personal Study" for that week. Explain that you will be providing some time before the video teaching next week for the group members to share their insights. Let them know sharing is optional, and it's not a problem if they can't get to these activities some weeks. It will still be beneficial for them to hear from the other participants and learn what they discovered.

LEADING THE DISCUSSION TIME

Now that the group is engaged, watch the video and respond with some directed small-group discussion. Encourage the group members to participate in the discussion, but make sure they know this is not mandatory for the group so that they don't feel pressured to come up with an answer. As the discussion progresses, follow up with comments such as, "Tell me more about that," or, "Why did you answer that way?" This will allow the group participants to deepen their reflections and invite a meaningful conversation in a nonthreatening way.

Note that you have been given multiple questions to use in each session, and you do not have to use them all or even follow them in order. Feel free to pick and choose questions based on the needs of your group or how the conversation is flowing. Also, don't be afraid of silence. Offering a question and allowing up to thirty seconds of silence is okay. This space allows people to think about how they want to respond and gives them time to do so.

As group leader, you are the boundary keeper for your group. Do not let anyone (yourself included) dominate the group time. Keep an eye out for group members who might be tempted to "attack" folks they disagree with or try to "fix" those having struggles. These kinds of behaviors can derail a group's momentum, so they need to be steered in a different direction. Model active listening and encourage everyone in your group to do the same. This will make your group time a safe space and create a positive community.

The group discussion leads to a closing time of individual reflection and prayer. Encourage the participants to review what they have learned and write down their thoughts to the "Respond" section. Close by taking a few minutes to pray together as a group.

Thank you again for taking the time to lead your group. You are making a difference in the lives of others and having an impact on the kingdom of God!

ABOUT THE AUTHOR

Dr. David Jeremiah is the founder of Turning Point, a ministry committed to providing Christians with sound Bible teaching relevant to today's changing times through radio and television broadcasts, audio series, books, and live events. Dr. Jeremiah's common-sense teaching on topics such as family, prayer, worship, angels, and biblical prophecy forms the foundation of Turning Point.

David and his wife, Donna, reside in El Cajon, California, where he serves as the senior pastor of Shadow Mountain Community Church. David and Donna have four children and twelve grandchildren.

In 1982, Dr. Jeremiah brought the same solid teaching to San Diego television that he shares weekly with his congregation. Shortly thereafter, Turning Point expanded its ministry to radio. Dr. Jeremiah's inspiring messages can now be heard worldwide on radio, television, and the internet.

Because Dr. Jeremiah desires to know his listening audience, he travels nationwide holding ministry rallies that touch the hearts and lives of many people. According to Dr. Jeremiah, "At some point in time, everyone reaches a turning point; and for every person, that moment is unique, an experience to hold onto forever. There's so much changing in today's world that sometimes it's difficult to choose the right path. Turning Point offers people an understanding of God's Word as well as the opportunity to make a difference in their lives."

Dr. Jeremiah has authored numerous books, including *Overcomer, The Book of Signs, A Life Beyond Amazing, People Are Asking . . . Is This the End?, Escape the Coming Night (Revelation), The Handwriting on the Wall (Daniel), Overcoming Loneliness, Prayer—The Great Adventure, God in You (Holy Spirit), When Your World Falls Apart, Slaying the Giants in Your Life, Hope for Today, Captured by Grace, Signs of Life, I Never Thought I'd See the Day!, God Loves You: He Always Has—He Always Will, Agents of the Apocalypse, Agents of Babylon, Daily in His Presence,* and *The God You May Not Know.*

ALSO FROM
DR. DAVID JEREMIAH

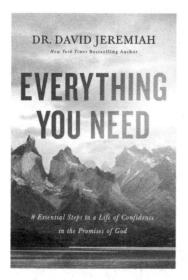

Our world is full of greater pressures and demands than ever before: relational pressure, time pressure, financial pressure, political pressure, and more. But you don't need to feel ill-equipped for the journey of life. That's because God Himself has already equipped you to overcome whatever comes your way. Though you may not even realize it yet, God has given you everything you will ever need not just to survive, but to thrive.

In *Everything You Need*, author and beloved Bible teacher Dr. David Jeremiah uses 2 Peter 1:3–11 to show you the path to spiritual and personal transformation. When God's power is unleashed in you, it enables you "to tread upon the heights" (Hab. 3:19). As His power is transmitted to you through His great and precious promises, you'll be increasingly transformed into the person you were created to be—someone who can successfully navigate the pressures of life with confidence and grace.

God Designed You for Victory

In this book and six-session video Bible study, bestselling author Dr. David Jeremiah uses Paul's instructions in Ephesians 6:10–18—his command for us to overcome the forces of evil by putting on the armor of God—to lay out a pathway for spiritual victory.

We all know it's hard out there. Sometimes it feels like the world is ripping apart at the seams. Sometimes it feels like our hearts can't take any more hurt. But no matter what the world throws at us each day—anxiety, fear, confusion, temptation—we have a choice on how to respond. We can either concede defeat or live in the victory God has promised.

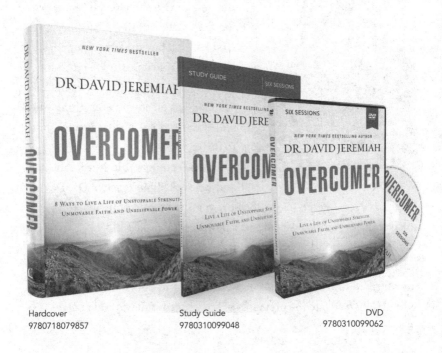

Hardcover
9780718079857

Study Guide
9780310099048

DVD
9780310099062

Available now at your favorite bookstore,
or streaming video on StudyGateway.com.

New Bible Study Series from Dr. David Jeremiah

The Jeremiah Bible Study Series captures Dr. David Jeremiah's forty-plus years of commitment to teaching the whole Word of God. Each volume contains twelve lessons for individuals and groups to explore what the Bible says, what it meant to the people at the time it was written, and what it means to us today. Out of his lifelong ministry of *delivering the unchanging Word of God to an ever-changing world*, Dr. Jeremiah has written this Bible-strong study series focused not on causes, current events, or politics, but on the solid truth of Scripture.

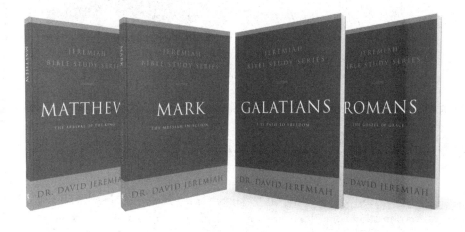

9780310091493	Matthew	9780310091554	John	9780310091646	1 Corinthians
9780310091516	Mark	9780310091608	Acts	9780310097488	2 Corinthians
9780310091530	Luke	9780310091622	Romans	9780310091660	Galatians

Available now at your favorite bookstore.
More volumes coming soon.

THOMAS NELSON
Since 1798

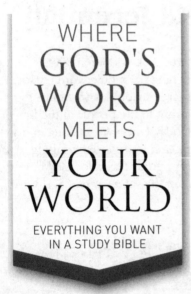

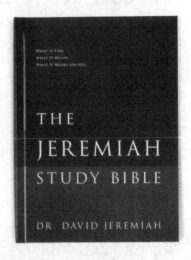

MORE THAN 500,000 PEOPLE
ARE USING **THE JEREMIAH STUDY BIBLE**

The Jeremiah Study Bible is comprehensive, yet easy to understand. More than forty years in the making, it is deeply personal and designed to transform your life. No matter your place or time in history, Scripture always speaks to the important issues of life. Hear God speak to you through studying His Word in *The Jeremiah Study Bible.*

NOW AVAILABLE IN:

- New Kings James Version
- Large Print NKJV
- New International Version

Request your Study Bible today:
www.DavidJeremiah.org/JSB

More Resources from Dr. Jeremiah

....

Overcomer

Discover the tools to become an Overcomer in every sense of the word—fully trusting God to prepare you for overcoming the trials and temptations that may cross your path. In this inspiring and practical book, Dr. David Jeremiah uses the armor of God that Paul describes in his letter to the Ephesian church to outline the path to victory.

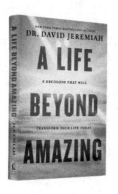

A Life Beyond Amazing

Discouraging headlines, personal adversity, and the toils of daily living often hold us back from living the life God has for us. In *A Life Beyond Amazing*, Dr. David Jeremiah urges us to move past these things, pointing us to a life of blessing beyond our comprehension. He shares nine traits, based on the fruit of the Spirit, that the Church is in need of today, teaching us that God desires for us to live beyond amazing while we await His return.

Stay connected to the teaching ministry of

DAVID JEREMIAH

Publishing | Radio | Television | Online

....

Take advantage of three great ways to let Dr. David Jeremiah give you spiritual direction every day!

Turning Points Magazine and Devotional

Receive Dr. Jeremiah's magazine,
Turning Points, each month:

- Thematic study focus
- 48 pages of life-changing reading
- Relevant articles
- Daily devotional readings and more!

Request *Turning Points* magazine today!
(800) 947-1993 | DavidJeremiah.org/Magazine

Daily Turning Point E-Devotional

Receive a daily e-devotion from Dr. Jeremiah that will strengthen your walk with God and encourage you to live the authentic Christian life.

Sign up for your free e-devotional today!
www.DavidJeremiah.org/Devo

Turning Point Mobile App

Access Dr. Jeremiah's video teachings, audio sermons, and more . . . whenever and wherever you are!

Download your free app today!
www.DavidJeremiah.org/App